FAMOUS COMPUTER INVENTIONS!
FROM THE PC TO MICRO COMPUTER FOR KIDS

Children's Computers & Technology Books

All Rights reserved. No part of this book may be reproduced or used in any way or form or by any means whether electronic or mechanical, this means that you cannot record or photocopy any material ideas or tips that are provided in this book.

Copyright 2016

Welcome to the futuristic computer age!

What do you know about computer innovations?

What can this amazing machine do for us?

What's the machine's worth?

The history of computers has been made possible by many inventors. A computer is a complex machine. Each of its complex parts is a separate invention.

A **microcomputer** is a small computer. It has a microprocessor as its central processing unit. The first computer was invented in 1945.

Computers of yesteryears were not personal and handy in any way.

During World War II, the massive and heavy machines were used. With their enormous size, team engineers kept them in use.

The Electronic Numerical Integrator Analyzer and Computer **(ENIAC)** was one of the most famous electronic digital computers.

It was built at the University of Pennsylvania. It weighed 30 tons! Can you imagine how enormous it was?

The massive earlier computers gradually changed into smaller sizes. As they got smaller, their capabilities significantly improved.

Computer buffs then program unassembled Personal Computers; thus, the PC's or microcomputers came to be. The early PC's were not that high-tech as today's modern PC's.

The **integrated circuit** and the **microprocessor** were the two technical innovations in the field of microelectronics that made possible the creations of personal Computers and microcomputers.

The miniaturization of computer-memory circuits were made possible by the integrated circuits.

The reduced sizes of the computer's CPU were made possible through the microprocessors. These CPU was transformed into its incredible smallest size.

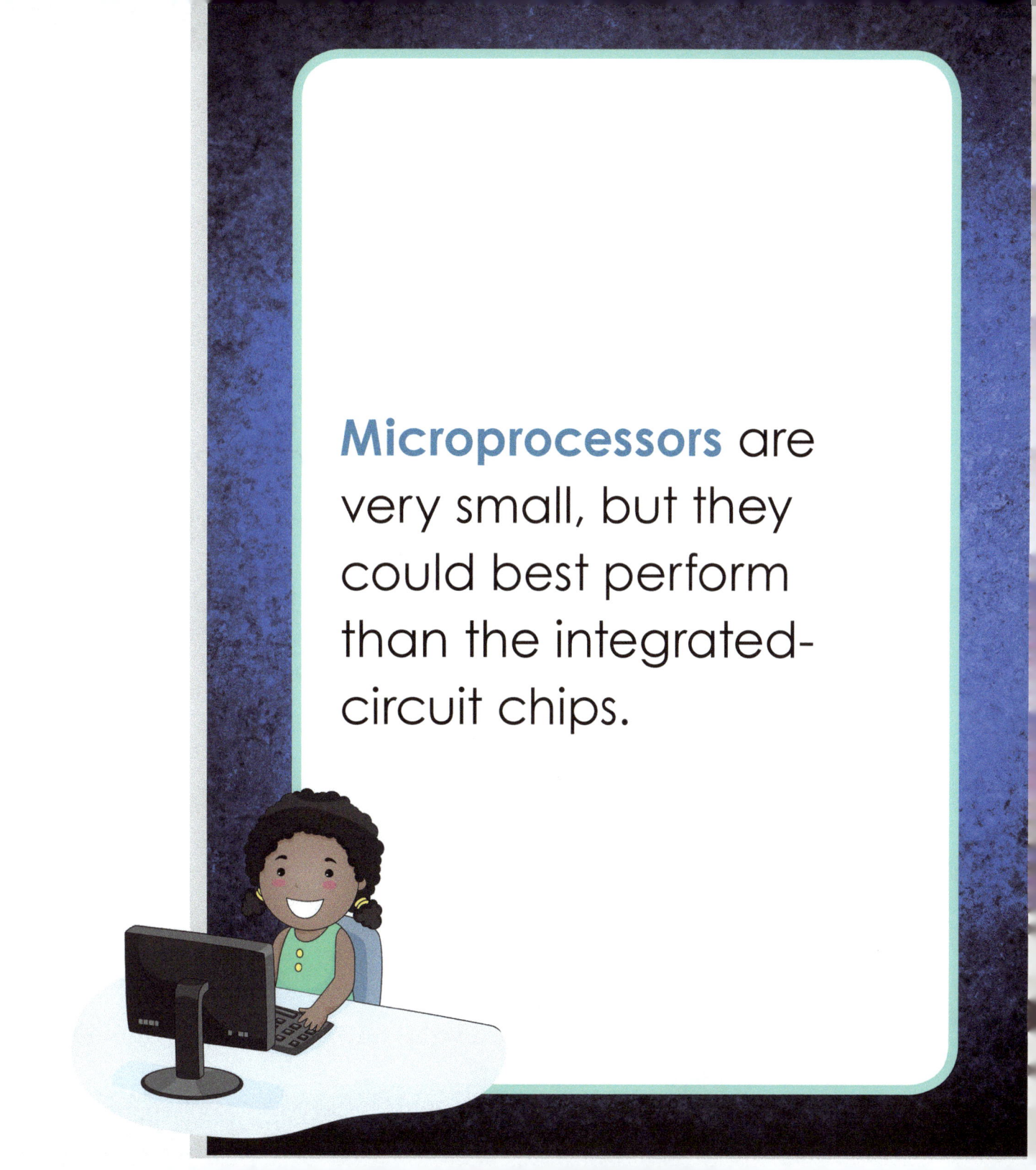

Microprocessors are very small, but they could best perform than the integrated-circuit chips.

Managing data, remembering information and running the computer's programs are all done by the microprocessors.

The evolution of Personal Computers was due to the invention of the microprocessor.

Today, the PC works amazingly with different modern gadgets. Numerous personal or desktop computers came to be. Examples are laptops, palmtops, portable PC's, Ipads and many more.

Today, Personal Computers can perform wide range of functions like word processing and editing photos. They perform useful tasks at home and at work. They are best buddies.

Modern life without them would be dull and slow. Laptops are becoming popular. But there are still people who are comfortable using desktop PCs. That is why there is still a big market for PCs.

Computers have become smaller in size, yet they are amazingly powerful. They can work at fast speed.

Many people take advantage of these incredible gadgets for they become user-friendly.

In 1968, the first **computer mouse** was introduced by Douglas Engelbert.

The **computer operating system** of the century was introduced by Microsoft in 1981.

It was in November 1985 that Microsoft windows were introduced. It has been known to be user-friendly.

In 1990, the father of Internet, Tim Berners-Lee, coined the phrase **World Wide Web**. The release of the first popular web Mosaic created a big impact on the use of the Internet.

Computers have brought the world closer. We can get in touch with our friends and loved ones in just one touch and click. Different types of personal computers came to be.

People all over the world enjoy using their mobile PC, laptops, netbooks, tablet PC and many other gadgets. Indeed, your personal computers are one of the greatest machines ever invented!

Lightning Source UK Ltd.
Milton Keynes UK
UKHW051859011122
411478UK00006B/54